MODERN RUSSIA

From Revolution to the Invasion of Ukraine

Craig E. Blohm

ReferencePoint Press®

San Diego, CA

About the Author

Craig E. Blohm has written numerous books and magazine articles for young readers. He and his wife, Desiree, reside in Tinley Park, Illinois.

For more information, contact:
ReferencePoint Press, Inc.
PO Box 27779
San Diego, CA 92198
www.ReferencePointPress.com

Picture Credits:
Cover: Shutterstock.com
4: Shutterstock.com
5: Shutterstock.com
8: Maury Aaseng
12: agefotostock/Alamy Stock Photo
14: World History Archive/Alamy Stock Photo
16: Science History Images/Alamy Stock Photo
21: Science History Images/Alamy Stock Photo
24: World History Archive/Alamy Stock Photo
27: Historical Images Archive/Alamy Stock Photo
31: World History Archive/Alamy Stock Photo
33: CPA Media Pte Ltd/Alamy Stock Photo
36: Pictorial Press Ltd/Alamy Stock Photo
41: Pictorial Press Ltd/Alamy Stock Photo
42: History and Art Collection/Alamy Stock Photo
45: Everett Collection Historical/Alamy Stock Photo
51: Kees Metselaar/Alamy Stock Photo
55: Associated Press
56: Pictorial Press Ltd/Alamy Stock Photo

LIBRARY OF CONGRESS CATALOGING-IN-PUBLICATION DATA

Names: Blohm, Craig E., 1948- author.
Title: Modern Russia : from revolution to the invasion of Ukraine / by Craig E. Blohm.
Description: San Diego, CA : ReferencePoint Press, 2024. | Includes bibliographical references and index.
Identifiers: LCCN 2022061212 (print) | LCCN 2022061213 (ebook) | ISBN 9781678205805 (library binding) | ISBN 9781678205812 (ebook)
Subjects: LCSH: Russia (Federation)--Economic conditions--Juvenile literature. | Soviet Union--History--Juvenile literature. | Russia (Federation)--History--1991---Juvenile literature.
Classification: LCC HC340.12 .B5956 2024 (print) | LCC HC340.12 (ebook) | DDC 330.947--dc23/eng/20230120
LC record available at https://lccn.loc.gov/2022061212
LC ebook record available at https://lccn.loc.gov/2022061213

CONTENTS

IMPORTANT EVENTS IN THE HISTORY OF MODERN RUSSIA

1825 1850 1875 1900 1925

1848
Philosophers Karl Marx and Friedrich Engels publish *The Communist Manifesto*.

1870
Founder of Soviet Russia Vladimir Ilyich Lenin is born.

1878
Joseph Stalin, Soviet dictator for a quarter century, is born.

1905
Revolution forces Czar Nicholas II to draft a Russian constitution.

1914
World War I begins.

1917
Revolutions in February and October remove the czar and establish Communist rule in Russia.

1918
A violent anti-revolution repression called the Red Terror begins; Bolsheviks ultimately kill as many as 1.3 million people.

1922
The Union of Soviet Socialist Republics (USSR) is formed.

1923
Lenin dies, leading to Stalin's takeover as head of the USSR.

1932
Famine in the Soviet Union causes millions of deaths.

1962
The Cuban missile crisis brings the world to the brink of nuclear war.

2022
Russia invades Ukraine, launching a months-long unprovoked and devastating war.

1945
The Soviet Union consolidates power over Eastern Europe at the end of World War II.

1939
World War II begins.

1991
The Soviet Union collapses.

1940 **1960** **1980** **2000** **2020**

1947
The Cold War between East and West begins.

2014
Russian forces occupy Crimea in southern Ukraine.

1985
As president, Mikhail Gorbachev initiates the ill-fated reforms of glasnost and perestroika.

2000
Vladimir Putin elected president of Russia.

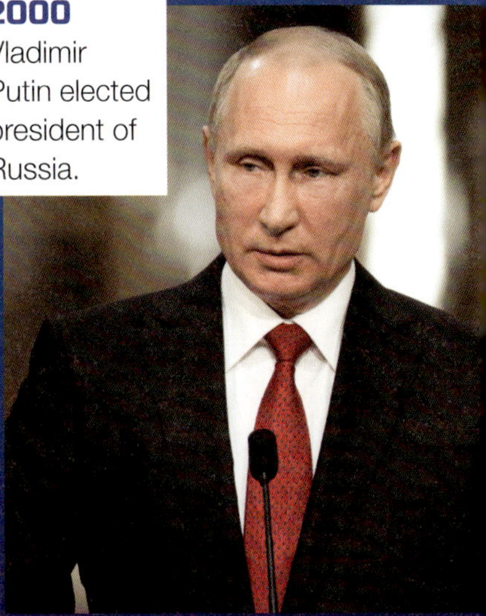

1943
German occupation forces are defeated in the Battle of Stalingrad.

Russia: Vision of a Communist World

By the middle of the nineteenth century, a revolution had forever changed the world. It was not a revolution of clashing armies or political upheaval but a transformation in the way nations created products and wealth for their citizens. Known as the Industrial Revolution, between 1760 and 1840 it shifted the economic power of Great Britain and the United States from crafting goods in homes and small workshops to massive urban factories that used machines to make products more quickly and cheaply.

The advances of the Industrial Revolution were not achieved without some undesirable consequences. Workers toiled long hours for little pay, laboring in filthy and unsafe conditions. Children as young as seven or eight years old were employed in the factories, leaving them no opportunity to attend school or play. In contrast, the ruling class that owned the factories reaped the benefits of the workers' labor, amassing great wealth in the process. The fact that this system, called capitalism, was driven by class inequality was not lost on a German philosopher named Karl Marx.

Marx believed that oppressed workers would one day rise up and take control of the factories for their own benefit. He envisioned a society based on common ownership of the means and rewards of industry, a concept known as social-

> **"Working men of all countries, unite!"[1]**
>
> —German philosopher Karl Marx

ism or, when achieved by violent revolution, communism. In *The Communist Manifesto*, Marx's most famous work, his rallying cry was, "Working men of all countries, unite!"[1] Marx predicted that communism would ultimately vanquish capitalism, but first capitalism would dominate the world's economy. Some countries, however, remained locked in their preindustrial societies. One of these countries was Russia.

Lenin's Revolution

In the late nineteenth century, Russia was a land of powerful monarchs called czars, who ruled over a vast nation made up mostly of peasants. Modern manufacturing technology had made few inroads into Russian society. The peasants remained poor, while the czar lived in opulent palaces. It was a nation destined for revolution.

In the early twentieth century, the Russian Empire was shattered by a series of rebellions, beginning in 1905 with worker strikes and military revolts. In October 1917 Vladimir Lenin, a disciple of Marx's Communist philosophy, led his Bolshevik Party in a rebellion against the reigning czar, Nicholas II. The Bolshevik Revolution ended the Russian monarchy and thrust Lenin into power.

A Communist Empire

Lenin seized control of Russia's industrial and agricultural assets and decreed that public lands be transferred to the people. In 1922 the Union of Soviet Socialist Republics (also known as the Soviet Union or USSR) was formed. It consisted of Russia, Belorussia, Ukraine, and Transcaucasia. At its height from the mid-1950s to 1991, it would encompass fifteen republics and about one-seventh of the earth's land surface.

Lenin ruled until his death in 1924 and was succeeded by Joseph Stalin, general secretary of the Communist Party. Under

Stalin's regime, communism spread throughout eastern Europe, but its growth was marked by harsh, authoritarian control leading to social unrest, brutal treatment of dissidents, and forced labor camps called gulags. After World War II the world entered a period known as the Cold War, pitting the Soviet Union against the United States and other Western powers in an ideological struggle. Tensions between East and West flared in 1962 when Russian missiles were discovered in Cuba, leading to a showdown between the United States and the Soviet Union. The missiles were ultimately removed, peacefully ending the threat of a nuclear war.

Communism's Failure

Although Lenin had predicted that communism would replace capitalism, the inherent weaknesses of the Communist system—ruthless totalitarianism, inefficient economic policies, and suppressed human rights—brought its downfall. On December 31, 1991, the Soviet Union ceased to exist, ending sixty-nine years of a political and social experiment that could not sustain itself in the modern world. Reborn as the Russian Federation, it was headed by a series of presidents who enacted policies that turned Russia away from its Communist basis. But corrupt Russian oligarchs (wealthy businesspersons) and military operations in Chechnya and Afghanistan kept the world wary of the former Communist nation. In 2022 Russian president Vladimir Putin sent troops into Ukraine, falsely declaring that the republic had always been a part of Russia. Ukrainian forces fought back, denying Putin a swift victory and forcing a drawn-out war.

The history of modern Russia is one of failed expectations, starving peasants, brutal terror against political rivals, and nuclear posturing. The collapse of communism left the door open for Russia to enter the twenty-first century as a peaceful nation. Putin's quest to return Russia to its former status as a world power may ultimately hinge on the outcome of the Ukraine war. Time will tell if the former empire, shattered by revolution and weakened by a failed system of Marxist ideology, can recapture its years of glory.

CHAPTER ONE

Empire and Revolution

On the morning of May 14, 1896, a bright sun glistened off five golden domes atop Dormition Cathedral within the Kremlin, the citadel that was the seat of the czar's government in Moscow. Inside the historic cathedral, thousands of candles illuminated colorful frescoes as priests solemnly attended the crowning of Russia's new czar, Nicholas II. Seated on a diamond-encrusted throne, Nicholas was presented with the Scepter and Imperial Orb, symbols of the czar's power over his subjects. He next received the bejeweled Great Imperial Crown. As church bells pealed across Moscow, a deacon announced the reign of "Nicholas Alexandrovich, Emperor and Autocrat of all Russia."[2]

But a few days after the coronation, tragedy marred the joy of the royal festivities. Nearly thirteen hundred people died and thousands were injured as a crowd rushed to acquire free coronation souvenirs. Some saw this as an ominous portent for the new czar; one newspaper proclaimed, "This means trouble! This reign will bring no good!"[3] Nicholas was the eighteenth emperor of the Romanov dynasty, which had reigned for three hundred years. He would be the last czar to rule over Russia.

Leading a Vast Empire

Romanov czars occupied the Russian throne during the seventeenth to early twentieth centuries. Some were capable and visionary monarchs, while others were emotionally or intellectually unsuited for the task. Whether effective or incompetent, the czars often ruled the empire with an iron fist and an inclination toward cruelty. Under the Romanovs, the Russian Empire expanded, and by the end of the nineteenth century its population had increased to 125 million people. Class divisions kept the czar at the top of Russian society, ruling the empire with absolute power and accountable only to God. At the bottom of society were the rural peasants, working the land as serfs for rich nobles.

In 1861 serfdom was abolished, freeing the peasants from servitude to their landlords. But they were still burdened with high taxes, a scarcity of land to farm, and constant hunger. Peasants were required to give a certain portion of their crops for export, often leaving little to feed their family. The years 1891 and 1892 saw a devastating famine cause the deaths of some four hundred thousand Russian peasants. The czar at the time, Alexander III, downplayed the disaster and refused to halt the export of grain that could have fed the starving masses. When Alexander died in 1894, his son Nicholas II took the throne.

A Weak Leader

Nicholas was emotionally and politically ill equipped to lead the nation and dreaded his ascent to the throne, lamenting, "I am not prepared to be a czar. I never wanted to become one. I know nothing of the business of ruling."[4] One thing Nicholas believed in, however, was the divine right of autocratic rule. A group of local administrators once petitioned him, seeking to gain more influence in running the government. He curtly

"I am not prepared to be a czar. I never wanted to become one. I know nothing of the business of ruling."[4]

—Czar Nicholas II

Nicholas II, the eighteenth emperor of the Romanov dynasty, would be the last czar to rule over Russia.

rebuked them, ridiculing their ideas as "senseless dreams."[5] Nicholas's blunt dismissal of the people's aspirations for a representative government began to fuel political opposition to the Russian autocracy.

By the turn of the twentieth century, life for the Russian working class was getting worse. Peasants who could not make a living farming migrated to the cities, where factories spawned by the Industrial Revolution offered some hope of work. Conditions in the Russian factories were appalling. "Unventilated working areas were filled with noxious fumes," writes historian Orlando Figes. "Shopfloors were crammed with dangerous machinery: there were frequent accidents. . . . Many factory owners treated workers like serfs."[6] Labor strikes occurred with increasing frequency, and worker demonstrations targeted factory owners and the czar as well. As the nineteenth century neared its end, revolution was looming.

Organizing for Revolution

In March 1898 a group of revolutionaries formed the Russian Social Democratic Labour Party (RSDLP) to promote the ideas of German philosopher Karl Marx. According to Marx's political treatise, *The Communist Manifesto*, the working class, or proletariat, would one day rise up and seize power from the industry owners, who were part of the middle class, or bourgeoisie. All factories and farmland would be given to the people, who would abolish the government and take control of their own destiny. This be-

> **"Unventilated working areas were filled with noxious fumes. Shop-floors were crammed with dangerous machinery: there were frequent accidents. . . . Many factory owners treated workers like serfs."[6]**
>
> —Historian Orlando Figes

came known as the dictatorship of the proletariat, which would create a society where economic classes no longer existed. It was the main element of the philosophy Marx called communism.

The RSDLP held its first meeting, or congress, in 1898. Other than publication of a manifesto stating the doctrines of the party, little was accomplished. Five of the nine delegates were later arrested, accused of plotting against the czar. Undaunted by persecution, the revolutionaries convened a second congress in 1903. One of the delegates was a Marxist revolutionary who would change the course of Russian history and set it on a path to becoming the world's first Communist nation.

Lenin and the Rise of the Bolsheviks

Vladimir Ilyich Ulyanov (better known by his revolutionary pseudonym, Lenin) was born in 1870, the son of bourgeois parents. His uneventful early years were shattered when his brother

Mutiny on the *Potemkin*

The battleship *Potemkin* was the flagship of Russia's Black Sea Fleet in 1905, but morale aboard the vessel did not match its exalted status. The food on the *Potemkin* was rotten, the ship was cramped and filthy, and the officers were cruel taskmasters. When the crew refused to eat their maggot-filled rations, the ship's second-in-command ordered thirty sailors to be executed.

Revolutionary ideas had been quietly circulating among several of the *Potemkin*'s crew, and the execution order sparked a rebellion. Two sailors, Afanasy Matyushenko and Grigory Vakulinchuk, confiscated weapons and led a mutiny in which seven officers, including the captain, were killed. Vakulinchuk was also fatally shot during the battle, which ended with the mutineers in charge of the *Potemkin*. The victorious sailors sailed the ship to the Ukrainian port of Odesa under a red flag of revolution. The rebellion, however, was soon put down by the czar's troops. The mutiny on the *Potemkin* is often regarded as the first event in the Revolution of 1905 and, ultimately, the Revolution of 1917 that ended czarist rule in Russia.

Aleksandr was executed in 1887 for taking part in a plot to assassinate czar Alexander III. His brother's death started Lenin on the road to political activism. Intending to study law, he enrolled at Kazan University, a state-run school. But as the brother of a would-be assassin, he aroused the suspicions of the czar's authorities: his every move was watched. Three months after enrolling, Lenin was expelled because of his presence at a student protest. He spent several years studying law and revolutionary politics, including Marx's philosophy, on his own. When he was eventually allowed to take the law exam, he passed with honors. But Lenin's career as a lawyer was short and unremarkable, for he was more concerned with revolution than the law.

In 1903 Lenin attended the second congress, at which two factions emerged over disagreements about the method for attaining the party's revolutionary goals. One faction, the Mensheviks (Russian for "minority"), advocated a slow, natural progression from capitalism toward communism that would ultimately displace the ruling class. Lenin led the other group, called the Bolsheviks ("majority"), which insisted that an elite, professional

The German philosopher Karl Marx (center) is depicted with a page of his political treatise, The Communist Manifesto.

The End of a Dynasty

In the early nineteenth century, the Russian city of Yekaterinburg was an industrial center and the main locale for mining Russian gold. But in 1918 it became the place where the Romanov dynasty of czars came to a violent end.

When Nicholas II abdicated his throne during the Revolution of 1917, the Bolsheviks faced the problem of what to do with the deposed czar and his family. It was decided to move them to the Ipatiev House in Yekaterinburg, a mansion once owned by a gold dealer. There Nicholas, his wife, Alexandra, and five children remained prisoners of the revolution.

In the early morning hours of July 17, 1918, the family was awakened and told to prepare for another move. They were taken to a basement room to await transportation. Instead, a group of armed men burst into the room and began firing at the prisoners with pistols. Within minutes, Nicholas and his family were dead, murdered by Bolsheviks who feared that royal sympathizers were coming to rescue the czar.

The bodies were buried in an unmarked grave in a nearby forest. The royal remains were not discovered until after the fall of the Soviet Union.

revolutionary force was needed to immediately and forcefully bring about the dictatorship of the proletariat. Lenin's faction gained control of the revolutionary movement, and he spent the next several years traveling throughout Europe, meeting and planning with other revolutionaries.

War and Protest

While Lenin was abroad, Nicholas was encountering problems both foreign and domestic. In 1904 war broke out between Russia and Japan over which nation should exert control over Manchuria, a Chinese territory. The conflict ended in a crushing defeat for Russia and created even more doubts about the czar's ability to lead the nation. At home, life for most Russians remained difficult. Peasant farmers could not grow enough crops, resulting in continued food shortages. Soon the urban population soared as more people left the farms to look for work in factories, leading to severely overcrowded living conditions.

On January 22, 1905, a massive demonstration took place in Russia's capital city of St. Petersburg. Thousands of striking workers, many accompanied by their wives and children, marched toward the czar's Winter Palace to present Nicholas with demands for government reform. This peaceful demonstration was met by the czar's imperial soldiers, who had orders to disperse the crowd. The troops opened fire, killing around two hundred protesters and wounding hundreds more. The horror of the massacre was matched only by its futility: Nicholas was not at the palace on that day, a day that came to be known as Bloody Sunday.

Reaction to Bloody Sunday was swift. Hundreds of thousands of Russian workers went out on strike to protest the government's brutal suppression of the march. In rural areas, peasant protests against their landlords spread across the empire. Local councils called soviets were formed to organize revolutionary activism among workers. Nicholas made no public statement about Bloody Sunday, although in his diary he described that event as "painful

The czar's soldiers brutally attack protesters during a demonstration in the Russian capital, St. Petersburg. Approximately two hundred protesters were killed and hundreds more were wounded on a day that came to be known as Bloody Sunday.

> **"The revolution has already begun."[8]**
>
> **—Minister to Czar Nicholas**

and sad."[7] But he could no longer ignore the will of his people to have a voice in the government. When one of his ministers told Nicholas that he had to act to quell the protests, the czar told him, "One would think that you are afraid a revolution will break out." The minister replied, "The revolution has already begun."[8]

Dress Rehearsal for Rebellion

Sparked by Bloody Sunday, the Revolution of 1905 was fueled by anger over the czar's autocratic policies and Russia's defeat in the war against Japan. Throughout the spring and summer of 1905, Russia was rocked by strikes, vandalism, and violent protests against the government. Lenin later called it a dress rehearsal for an even greater revolution to come. The violence was quelled after eight days, but by October railroads, factories, schools, and other essential services had been shut down by strikes.

Left with few options, Nicholas issued the October Manifesto, which gave Russians basic rights, such as freedom of speech and assembly, and the right to vote. An elected parliament, called the Duma, was established, and without its approval no new laws could be enacted. It was a victory for the Russian people, although still far from the freedom enjoyed by other European nations. The czar remained in control and could dissolve the Duma if he so chose. Still, the October Manifesto was the first step on the path to bringing Russia into the modern era. Nicholas, however, saw it as the end of his own era of power. "I feel that in signing this act," he told an adviser, "I have lost the crown. Now all is finished."[9] Nicholas was correct, but premature: it would take another twelve years, a world war, and two more revolutions for his words to come true.

War and Revolution

If Russia's war with Japan was humiliating, the next war was a disaster. In 1914 World War I (then called the Great War) broke out in Europe. Russia joined the war on the side of Great Britain and France, fighting against Germany and Austria-Hungary. Russia was unprepared for a conflict of such magnitude, lacking sufficient weapons and ammunition for its troops. To make matters worse, Nicholas decided to take command of Russia's military himself, a role for which he was not prepared. Indecisive on the battlefield, the czar knew nothing of military strategy and thus was blamed for every military setback.

By the end of the war, Russia had lost an estimated 1.8 million to 2.3 million soldiers. Civilian casualties totaled more than 400,000. Both liberals and conservatives in the Duma placed the blame for Russia's poor efforts in the war squarely on the shoulders of the czar. Meanwhile, rampant inflation and food shortages continued to plague the countryside. In February 1917 the first of two revolutions began to change the course of Russian history. Beginning in Petrograd (as St. Petersburg was renamed during the war), demonstrations of up to 150,000 peasants, striking workers, and women seeking equal rights marched in the streets. The czar's soldiers were ordered to break up the demonstrations. They killed as many as two hundred protesters. The next day, the soldiers, fed up with the czar and appalled at being ordered to shoot fellow Russians, joined the demonstrators. When Nicholas was informed by his generals that the army had turned against him, he knew that his reign was over. On March 2, 1917, Nicholas II gave up the throne, ending forever the rule of czars over the Russian Empire. A few days before his announcement, the Provisional Government had been formed to fill the void left by the czar's impending abdication. But opposition by the powerful Petrograd Soviet (which was more powerful than the government) would doom the new regime before the year was out.

CHAPTER TWO

Revolutionary Changes

On a railroad platform in Switzerland near the German border, thirty-two Russian revolutionaries climbed aboard a steam train that sat puffing on the tracks. It was March 27, 1917, and the group was about to embark on a trip home to Russia after spending years in exile abroad. Lenin was one of those exiles, and he was especially eager to return to Russia. He had heard about the February Revolution, and he knew it was time to fulfill his destiny.

On the first leg of the eight-day journey to Petrograd, the train passed through Germany, which was an enemy still fighting Russia in the Great War. The train was designated a "sealed" train, having special authority to travel through hostile nations unimpeded. In fact, Germany wanted the Bolsheviks to return home and promote the revolution, in the hopes of weakening Russia's war effort. During the grueling 2,000-mile (3,219 km) journey, Lenin spent his time aboard the train reading newspapers, pondering ideas about how the revolution should proceed, and talking with his fellow revolutionaries.

Shortly after eleven o'clock on a freezing April night, the train pulled into the Finland Station in Petrograd, which was festooned in red banners and packed with citizens, workers, and a navy honor guard. Cheers went up as Lenin exited the train, after which he addressed the crowd in support of the revolution against Russia's Provisional Government.

> When they [the Provisional Government] make sweet promises, you are being deceived in the same way that the entire Russian population is being deceived. The people need bread and land. They give you war and hunger—and the landowners still have all the land. . . . Comrades, we have to fight for a socialist revolution, fight to the end. Long live the world-wide social revolution![10]

Lenin was then ushered into an armored car and whisked off to Kschessinska Mansion, the former home of a Russian ballerina that had been commandeered by the Bolsheviks as their headquarters. It was in this lavish manor that Lenin would, for the first time, present his plan for revolution.

The April Theses

Some hours after Lenin reached Kschessinska, he addressed fellow Bolsheviks gathered in the elegant White Hall of the mansion. His fiery speech presented ten items for accomplishing the revolution that would turn Russia into the proletarian utopia that he envisioned. The main points of Lenin's plan included opposition to the Provisional Government, establishing the soviets as the only form of government, abolishing the police and the army, and placing all agricultural lands under control of local soviets. In his speech, Lenin declared that Russia was "passing from the first stage of the revolution . . . to its second stage, which must place power in the hands of the proletariat and the poorest sections of the peasantry."[11]

Lenin's plan came as a shock to the Bolsheviks, who had expressed conditional support of the Provisional Government. They followed Marx's theory that social change could only succeed after a nation became a modern industrial society in which the people demonstrated that they were capable of governing. Russia was nowhere near achieving that status, but Lenin believed that the

Vladimir Lenin returns to St. Petersburg (known at the time as Petrograd) following years in exile. He is cheered by the public as he waves to the crowd.

power of violent revolution could bring about his vision for Russian society. On April 7 the Bolshevik newspaper, *Pravda* (Russian for "Truth"), published a summary of Lenin's revolutionary declarations.

Meanwhile, the Provisional Government, led by lawyer and activist Alexander Kerensky, kept Russia in the increasingly unpopular and costly Great War. He ordered a disastrous offensive that resulted in some four hundred thousand Russian casualties. He also cracked down on Bolshevik protesters during four days of demonstrations in Petrograd known as the July Days. Many of the demonstrators were jailed, and others, including Lenin, were forced into exile. To many, it seemed that Lenin and the Bolsheviks had become too unpopular to regain their influence over Russian politics. But another revolution would soon sweep Lenin into power and change the world.

The Bolshevik Revolution

After the July Days, with the Russian economy devastated by the war, mass protests continued to rock Petrograd. In August,

Eyewitness to the Revolution

John Reed was an American journalist and activist who was sympathetic to the Bolshevik Revolution. Born in 1887, Reed ultimately identified with the socialist movement and wrote articles for *The Masses*, a socialist magazine. He became friends with Lenin and was instrumental in the creation of the Communist Party of America.

Reed is most remembered for his book *Ten Days That Shook the World*, about his experiences as a witness to the Bolshevik Revolution. In it, Reed recounts entering the Winter Palace with the Bolsheviks:

> Just inside a couple of soldiers stood on guard, but they said nothing. At the end of the corridor was a large, ornate room with gilded cornices and enormous crystal lustres [chandeliers]. . . . On both sides of the parqueted floor lay rows of dirty mattresses and blankets, upon which occasional soldiers were stretched out.
>
> The place was all a huge barrack, and evidently had been for weeks, from the look of the floor and walls. Machine guns were mounted on window-sills, rifles stacked between the mattresses.

Reed died of typhus at age thirty-two and was buried in the Kremlin, one of only three Americans to be interred there.

John Reed, *Ten Days That Shook the World*. New York: St. Martin's, 1997, pp. 67–68.

Russian army commander in chief General Lavr Kornilov assembled troops to subdue the unrest. But Kerensky viewed Kornilov's actions as an attempt to take over the government and relieved him of command. When the general defied the order and commanded his troops to advance, Kerensky enlisted the aid of the Petrograd Soviet, including members of the Red Guard, to put down Kornilov's attack. Without a shot being fired, Kornilov's attempted coup was thwarted. The incident illustrated the government's weakness, and it increased popular support for the Bolsheviks. By September they were the majority faction of the Petrograd Soviet, and other Russian soviets began welcoming the Bolsheviks.

For Lenin, hiding in Finland since the July Days, the time seemed right for the final revolution. "History will not forgive us," Lenin wrote to the Bolshevik Party's leadership committee, "if we do not assume power now."[12] He was frustrated that he was missing out on the growing revolutionary atmosphere in Petrograd. Wearing a disguise, Lenin secretly slipped back into the city, and on October 10 he called a late-night meeting of fellow Bolsheviks to discuss the revolution. At dawn a vote was taken, and the result sealed Russia's fate. The revolution would go forward.

Preparations for the revolution could not be kept secret, and soon talk of the impending insurrection spread throughout Petrograd. Indeed, soviets across Russia were increasing their own rebellious activities. On October 24 Kerensky ordered his military to shut down Lenin's revolutionary activities. Now the Bolsheviks had a reason to revolt, since they would be defending themselves from government forces. Under authority of the Bolshevik Military Revolutionary Committee, led by radical Leon Trotsky, the Red Guards (armed worker militias) took over government budlings, roads and bridges, electrical plants, and newspaper and telegraph offices. A confident Lenin published a notice "To the Citizens of Russia" on the morning of October 25, even before his victory was assured: "The Provisional Government has been deposed. . . . The cause for which the people have fought, namely, the immediate offer of a democratic peace, the abolition of landed proprietorship, workers' control over production, and the establishment of Soviet power—this cause has been secured. Long live the revolution of workers, soldiers and peasants!"[13]

"The Provisional Government has been deposed. . . . The cause for which the people have fought . . . has been secured. Long live the revolution of workers, soldiers and peasants!"[13]

—Vladimir Lenin

The final objective for the Bolsheviks was the Provisional Government's headquarters, Petrograd's Winter Palace. Bolshevik forces surrounded the massive building and waited for the order to attack. At about 9:40 p.m. on October 25, a loud boom echoed through the city. It was the cruiser *Aurora*, anchored nearby on the Neva River, firing a blank cannon shot, the signal to advance. As the Red Guard troops moved through the great halls and corridors, they encountered minimal resistance. Guarding the palace

In October of 1917, Bolshevik forces stormed the Winter Palace, headquarters of Russia's Provisional Government.

was a small group of defenders, including Cossacks (independent soldiers), teenage military cadets, and members of a volunteer Women's Battalion. Outnumbered, most of them surrendered or were quickly subdued. Only a few shots were fired, leading to an almost bloodless overtaking of the government headquarters.

Thirteen ministers, the last remnant of the Provisional Government (except for Kerensky, who—after a failed attempt to rally his troops for a counterattack—had abandoned his collapsing government and fled the country), were meeting in a dining room of the Winter Palace. A group of Red Guards burst into the room. "I am Antonov-Ovseyenko," the leader of the Red Guards shouted, "a representative of the Military Revolutionary Committee. I inform all you members of the Provisional Government that you are under arrest."[14] The ministers were imprisoned in Petrograd's Peter and Paul Fortress. It was the early morning of October 26, and before leaving the room, someone stopped the hands of an ornate mantel clock. The frozen hands pointed to 2:10 a.m.—the exact moment that everything changed for Russia.

Lenin in Charge

While Bolshevik troops were storming the Winter Palace, soviet delegates from across Russia were meeting to finalize the new revolutionary government. Representatives to the All-Russian Congress of Soviets met at the Smolny Institute, a concrete and stone building with tall columns and masonry arches. Originally built as a school for girls, in 1917 it served as the headquarters of the revolution. The discussions became heated, and delegates who opposed the revolution walked out, clearing the way for the Bolsheviks to vote for approval. The new government was called the Council of People's Commissars, and Lenin was elected its chair. The Bolshevik Party would soon rename itself the Communist Party.

Many observers gave the fledgling government little chance of success. But the delegates at the congress cheered when Lenin stepped up to the podium and declared, "We shall now proceed to construct the socialist order."[15] Lenin's promises of peace, bread, and land had become the rallying cry of the Revolution of 1917. Now he had to turn his promises into reality. Lenin laid out the agenda for the new government in a series of decrees. His

Lenin's Hanging Order

In the summer of 1918, an uprising of kulaks (wealthy landowners) took place in Penza, a town some 388 miles (624 km) southeast of Moscow. To make an example of the anti-revolutionary rebels, Lenin sent a telegram to Penza's Communist leaders, describing in vivid detail what should be done to the kulaks.

> Comrades! The uprising by the five kulak volosts [communities] must be mercilessly suppressed. The interest of the entire revolution demands this, for we are now facing everywhere the "final decisive battle" with the kulaks. We need to set an example.
>
> 1. You need to hang (hang without fail, so that the people see) no fewer than 100 of the notorious kulaks, the rich and the bloodsuckers.
> 2. Publish their names.
> 3. Take all their grain from them.
> 4. Appoint the hostages—in accordance with yesterday's telegram.
>
> This needs to be done in such a way that the people for hundreds of versts [miles] around will see, tremble, know and shout: they are throttling and will throttle the bloodsucking kulaks.

V.I. Lenin, "Telegram to Comrades Kuraev, Bosh, Minkin, and Other Penza Communists, August 11, 1918," Marxists Internet Archive, 2008. www.marxists.org.

> **"The right to use the land shall be accorded to all citizens of the Russian state (without distinction of sex) desiring to cultivate it by their own labor."[16]**
>
> **—Lenin's Decree on Land**

Decree on Peace called for an immediate end to the hostilities of the Great War and the beginning of peace negotiations. This led to Russia's withdrawal from the war, made official by the Treaty of Brest-Litovsk in March 1918. The treaty forced Russia to surrender more than 1 million square miles (2.6 million sq. km) of territory, including much of its industrial and natural resources, to Germany. Lenin's Decree on Land abolished private ownership of land held by wealthy nobles. The decree stated, "The right to use the land shall be accorded to all citizens of the Russian state (without distinction of sex) desiring to cultivate it by their own labor."[16] Russian peasants would finally have their own land on which to grow food for their families.

Lenin's decrees gave the Russian people the three things they had longed for. But a storm was brewing, and more changes were to come.

Civil War and the Red Terror

Not everyone in Russia was satisfied with the new government. Many who expected it to be a political system with multiple parties and free elections soon realized that the Bolsheviks were actually the only power in Russia. Opposing Lenin's government was the White Army, a loose coalition of several armed forces led by former czarist generals, including Kornilov. Lenin's forces, called the Red Army (an expansion of the Red Guards), was made up of workers and peasants and commanded by Trotsky. The Red Army was better organized than the White Army, which suffered from lack of coordination and little support from the people. Throughout 1918 and 1919 the two military forces fought in numerous battles across Russia and neighboring territories. In November 1920 the Red Army gained a decisive victory in the Crimean Peninsula, striking a fatal blow to the White Army. Intermittent fighting continued until 1922, when the White Army finally gave up, ending a war

Leon Trotsky (center) commanded what was known as the Red Army, which was made up of workers and peasants.

that produced more than 8 million casualties and a brutal reign of terror instigated by Lenin.

Opposition to the new government triggered a nearly lethal encounter for Lenin. On August 30, 1918, he had just finished giving a speech at a factory when a woman named Fanny Kaplan fired three shots at him with a pistol. One bullet struck Lenin in the neck, a serious wound that could have killed the Communist leader. But he survived and, a few days later, wrote, "It is necessary secretly—and urgently—to prepare the terror."[17] Lenin's order resulted in the Red Terror, a program of using mass murder to eliminate the enemies of the new Communist government, including intellectuals, clergy, anti-revolutionaries, criminals, and numerous others. Carried out by the Cheka (Lenin's secret police), up to 2 million people were executed during the Red Terror, which lasted from September 1918 to the end of the civil war in 1922.

"It is necessary secretly—and urgently—to prepare the terror."[17]

—Vladimir Lenin

End of an Era

On December 30, 1922, Russia and three other Soviet Socialist Republics (Belorussia, Ukraine, and Transcaucasia) signed documents creating the USSR, the world's first Communist state. It was the realization of Lenin's dream of a nation governed by his interpretation of Marx's classless socialist society. But Lenin would not live long enough to guide the direction of his creation.

In May 1922 Lenin suffered the first of three strokes that would ultimately end his life. His brain affected, and suffering partial paralysis, Lenin could no longer engage in political discourse. In March 1923 a final stroke robbed Lenin of his ability to speak and left him bedridden. For a time it appeared that he was getting better, but it was only a temporary improvement. Lenin died on January 21, 1924. His embalmed body was placed in a glass sarcophagus at the Kremlin in Moscow, which had succeeded St. Petersburg as the nation's capital in March 1918. To this day millions of people visit the Kremlin each year to pay their respects to the founder of the Soviet Union.

Before his death, Lenin was able to dictate a testament, in which he set forth his hopes for the future of the Soviet Union. In it he told of a possible split in the Communist Party, warning of one man who could destroy the nation if he acquired too much power. Ironically, that man would succeed Lenin as the leader of the USSR, and in the process create a cruel regime of violence and terror of his own.

CHAPTER THREE

An Era of Terror and War

Joseph Vissarionovich Dzhugashvili was born in 1878 in Gori, Georgia, a province of the Russian Empire. He had a difficult youth. His mother and his alcoholic father beat him often, and they each had different plans for his future. His mother wanted him to become a priest and enrolled Joseph in the local religious school, but his father thought his son should follow in his footsteps as a cobbler. Joseph was bullied by other children for facial scars left by a bout of smallpox. His left arm did not grow as long as his right, and a carriage accident when he was eleven years old had left him with a limp that plagued him for the rest of his life. A tough, streetwise youth, Joseph adopted the nickname Koba, after the brash hero of a popular novel. When he later became a Bolshevik revolutionary, he took a name that he thought better represented himself: Koba became Stalin, the "Man of Steel."

Stalin soon began to associate with peers who embraced radical political ideas. He abandoned his priesthood studies and began reading revolutionary works, including Marx's *Communist Manifesto* and Lenin's writings. After Stalin's first meeting with Lenin in 1905, he joined the Bolshevik Party and was soon planning bank robberies to fund the party's revolutionary activities. Rising through the

Communist ranks, in 1922 he became general secretary of the Communist Party's Central Committee, attaining the considerable power that came with the office.

A struggle ensued over who would lead the Soviet Union after Lenin's death in 1924. Lenin had warned of Stalin's growing power, writing in his testament, "Stalin is too rude and this defect . . . becomes intolerable in a Secretary-General. That is why I suggest that the comrades think about a way of removing Stalin from that post and appointing another man in his stead."[18] But Stalin was able to prevail over the misgivings of his mentor, and by 1928 he had defeated his opponents to become the dictator of the Soviet Union.

Stalin's Five-Year Plans

The nation that Stalin now headed still lagged behind the rest of the industrialized world. Peasants using obsolete farm implements could not produce enough grain for the country's population, and factory workers were hampered by the lack of modern machinery. "We are fifty to one hundred years behind the advanced countries," Stalin said in a speech to Soviet industrial leaders. "We must close the gap in ten years. Either we do this or they will crush us."[19] To achieve this goal, Stalin initiated the first of a series of Five-Year Plans to bring the Soviet Union into the twentieth century.

Beginning in 1928, the first Five-Year Plan created a system of collective farms to modernize Soviet agriculture. Peasants were forced to work for a state-owned collective, or kolkhoz, instead of running their own private farms. On the collectives, farmers had access to better farming equipment, which allowed them to increase their agricultural crop yield. But the government controlled farm production, setting often unrealistic quotas and determining how much farmers

"We are fifty to one hundred years behind the advanced countries. We must close the gap in ten years. Either we do this or they will crush us."[19]

—Joseph Stalin

On state-owned collective farms, peasants had access to better farm equipment, such as tractors, which allowed them to improve crop yields. The peasants did not like the arrangement, however, because it gave the government too much power.

would be paid for their labor. The peasants hated the collective farm system. In protest, many destroyed their crops and killed their livestock rather than submit to the state.

Ordinary peasants were not the only protesters against the kolkhozes. Relatively prosperous farmers who owned livestock and managed large farms were known as kulaks. The Communist leadership condemned the kulaks as anti-revolutionaries and greedy exploiters of the poorer farmers. Stalin vowed to "carry out a resolute offensive against the kulaks, break their resistance, eliminate them as a class."[20] In 1929 he began a program of "dekulakization" to rid the Soviet Union of them by deportation and murder. An estimated 5 million kulaks were exiled to work camps called gulags in the frozen wilderness of Siberia. About thirty thousand others were summarily shot without any kind of legal proceedings.

In 1932 Stalin declared that the first Five-Year Plan had ended successfully one year ahead of schedule. Soviet heavy industry had made great strides forward, with new urban factories turning out tractors and other farm machinery. With the growing emphasis on manufacturing, the factories needed workers and the peasant farmers needed jobs. This led to a mass exodus as thousands of peasants left their farms to work in the cities. This, along with increased quotas for grain exports, poor growing seasons, and the ongoing elimination of the kulak class, caused farm output to fall precipitously. The result was starvation on a massive scale.

The Great Famine

The famine that began in 1932 was most strongly felt in the agricultural regions, including the Kazakh and Ukrainian Soviet republics. The inhabitants of these regions endured horrifying conditions during this period, as noted by an eyewitness: "It is for many months that most of the local families have nothing to put on the table. All the cellars were swept clean, not a single hen remained in the village. . . . The first who died of hunger were the men. Later on the children. And last of all, the women. But before they died, people often lost their senses and ceased to be human beings."[21]

One of the hardest-hit regions was Ukraine, where the famine was called the Holodomor, meaning "to kill by hunger." Ukrainians were forbidden to leave the republic to find food as Soviet police confiscated their crops and personal belongings. Starving peasants sent their children to beg for food on the village streets, and reports of cannibalism began to circulate. Hoarding even a small amount of grain was punishable by execution. Of the 5 million people who died of starvation across the Soviet Union, some 4 million were Ukrainians.

"It is for many months that most of the local families have nothing to put on the table. All the cellars were swept clean, not a single hen remained in the village."[21]

—Witness to the Great Famine

The Great Famine of 1932–1933 was a human-made disaster, created by Stalin's push for Soviet industrialization. Stalin played down the devastation, forbidding

A famine, called the Holodomor, meaning "to kill by hunger," forbade Ukrainians from leaving the republic to find food as Soviet police confiscated their crops. Of the 5 million people who died of starvation across the Soviet Union, some 4 million were Ukrainians. This family leaves home to search for food.

newspapers to print stories about the famine. He feared anything that could potentially taint his reputation and power and became convinced that his enemies were out to destroy him. Stalin took drastic measures to prevent any of this from occurring.

Stalin's Great Terror

The spark that set these measures in motion came in December 1934. On December 1 of that year, Sergei Kirov braved the cold weather in Leningrad (the new name of Petrograd, changed as a tribute to Lenin after his death) to walk to his office in the Smolny Institute. A friend of Stalin and the popular head of the Leningrad Soviet, Kirov was going to work on a speech he would give later that evening. Inside the building, he was approaching his office when a young man appeared out of the shadows and shot Kirov in the head, killing him instantly. When Stalin was told of Kirov's death, he appeared shocked, despite speculation that he had harbored doubts about Kirov's loyalty and had arranged the assassination himself. Involved or not, Stalin used the incident to begin eliminating his political enemies, real and imagined.

That same night, Stalin announced harsh punishment for anyone he deemed a traitor. Charges would be swiftly brought against suspects, no defense lawyers or appeals were allowed, and sentences (including execution) were to be immediately carried out. Thus began Stalin's Great Terror (also called the Great Purge). No one was exempt from persecution. Communist Party members, officers of the Red Army, intellectuals, artists, scientists, and ordinary citizens were apprehended and either executed or exiled to the gulags. The arrests and punishments were carried out by Stalin's much-feared secret police, the NKVD.

In the Gulag

Janusz Bardach was drafted into the Red Army in 1940, becoming a tank driver in World War II. An accident with his tank led to a court-martial and a ten-year sentence laboring at the gold mines of the Kolyma gulag. He describes working at Kolyma in his memoir, *Man Is Wolf to Man: Surviving the Gulag*.

> The oppressive work regimen was a form of torture in itself. Sometimes I thought hacking the cement-hard soil with a wrought-iron crowbar was unbearable. I felt the limits of my endurance approaching when I couldn't fulfill the norm [work quota]. . . . I thought about injuring myself as so many prisoners had done, hoping to win several days in the hospital.
>
> It was becoming more and more difficult to make the norm. Would I reach the day, as so many others had, when I'd look for food in the garbage piles? It was the most common form of degradation. Rummaging through the garbage, eating rancid scraps of meat, chewing on fish skeletons—such behavior was so common that no one noticed.

Bardach survived eight months of hard labor in Kolyma's gold mines. He later became a noted surgeon in Poland and the United States.

Janusz Bardach, *Man Is Wolf to Man: Surviving the Gulag*. Berkeley: University of California Press, 1998, pp. 220–21.

From 1936 to 1938 former party officials and their associates were subjected to staged trials, where guilty verdicts were certain. Intimidation, threats against family members, and torture were routinely used to extract false confessions from the suspects. Among those sentenced to death were Grigory Zinoviev and Lev Kamenev, high-ranking party members who, despite helping Stalin rise to power, were later labeled as traitors. Even Leon Trotsky, who had helped Lenin carry out the revolution only to ultimately fall out of favor with the Bolsheviks, was not spared. He was living in exile in Mexico when he was tracked down and assassinated.

At least 750,000 people were killed during the Great Terror. Millions more were exiled to the gulags, where death by starvation or overwork awaited. Stalin even executed about 80 percent of the Soviet Union's generals, leaving the country without the military leadership it would desperately need in the coming years.

A New World War

In the summer of 1939, the world was on the brink of a new and catastrophic global war. After Germany's humiliating defeat in World War I, Chancellor Adolf Hitler had rebuilt his nation's military into a formidable fighting machine. As leader of the Nazi Party, Hitler was poised to conquer Europe and eliminate anyone who did not live up to the ideals of the so-called Aryan (White) race. Stalin feared the German army would invade Russia once the war began, so he authorized his foreign minister, Vyacheslav Molotov, to make a deal with Molotov's German counterpart, Joachim von Ribbentrop.

At a meeting in Moscow on August 24, the ministers signed a nonaggression pact agreeing that the two nations would not attack each other. The pact assured Hitler that he could proceed with his war without having to fight the Soviet Union. For Stalin, it allayed his fears of a German invasion. A secret part of the pact delineated how Europe would be divided once the inevitable

> **"I can guarantee on my word of honor that the Soviet Union will not betray its partner."[22]**
>
> **—Joseph Stalin**

war began, creating German and Soviet spheres of influence. "I can guarantee on my word of honor," Stalin said after the signing, "that the Soviet Union will not betray its partner."[22] Hitler, however, gave no such assurance. The German-Soviet Nonaggression Pact was intended to last for ten years. Hitler would breach it in less than two.

Germany Invades the Soviet Union

After invading Poland in September 1939, Nazi Germany had, by mid-1941, conquered the northern European country of Norway, as well as most of western Europe, including Belgium, France, Netherlands, and Denmark. Hitler next turned his attention eastward, toward the abundant natural resources and industrial might of the Soviet Union. Confident in the ability of his powerful army, Hitler began amassing some 3 million troops along the Soviet Union's border. The invasion, codenamed Operation Barbarossa, began on June 22, 1941, as German troops and tanks

The German invasion of the Soviet Union, codenamed Operation Barbarossa, began on June 22, 1941.

John Steinbeck's Russian Journal

Renowned American author John Steinbeck and war photographer Robert Capa visited Stalingrad in 1948 with the idea of revealing the lives of ordinary Russians in words and photographs. Steinbeck described a devastated city with a resilient population.

> We would watch out of the windows of our [hotel] room, and from behind a . . . pile of rubble would suddenly appear a girl, going to work in the morning, putting the last little touches to her hair with a comb. She would be dressed neatly. . . . How they could do it we have no idea. How they could live underground and still keep clean and proud and feminine.
>
> We wanted to see and photograph the famous Stalingrad tractor factory. For it was in this factory that the men had continued to build tanks when the Germans were firing on them. And when the Germans got too close, they put down their tools, and went out and defended the factory, and then went back and continued working. . . . Here in the factory, which had been defended by its own workers, and where those same workers were still building tractors, could be found the spirit of the Russian defense.

John Steinbeck, *A Russian Journal*. New York: Bantam, 1948, pp. 120, 126, 127.

poured across the border and the Luftwaffe (air force) bombed Soviet military targets. The Germans caught the Red Army totally unprepared. Stalin was so traumatized that it was a week before he could react to the news of the invasion. The Soviet military sustained nearly 750,000 casualties in the first eighteen days of the German advance.

Leningrad and Stalingrad

Soon after the invasion, the German forces set their sights on the city of Leningrad, where factories were turning out weapons for the Red Army. A German victory would be a blow to the Soviet war machine as well as a propaganda triumph for Germany. By September 8 the Germans had surrounded Leningrad, cutting off supply routes to the city. As the Red Army struggled against the German offensive, citizens of Leningrad began fortifying the city with sandbags, trenches, and anti-tank barriers. Rather than risk his troops in a ground assault, Hitler decided to lay siege to the city and starve the inhabitants to death.

For months, then years, Leningrad held out against German artillery and bombers. A few meager supplies managed to reach the city. But starvation and cold took their toll, and in 1942 alone, some six hundred thousand people died. By 1943 the Red Army had opened up a supply route, and more food and supplies began to flow into Leningrad. Early the next year, an offensive by more than 1 million Soviet soldiers pushed back the German army. After 872 days, the siege of Leningrad was broken on January 27, 1944. An estimated 1.5 million Soviet civilians and soldiers lost their lives in the siege.

While Leningrad fought for its very existence, another Soviet city was also fending off a German advance. In August 1942 German forces attacked Stalingrad, an industrial center in the south of the Soviet Union. Brutal street fighting, along with massive artillery and aerial bombing, made Stalingrad one of the bloodiest battles in history. With some three hundred thousand German troops fighting within the city, the Red Army launched a counteroffensive in November 1942. The Soviets managed to surround the Germans, cutting off their supplies and finally forcing surrender on February 2, 1942. In the seven-month battle for Stalingrad, the German military suffered more than eight hundred thousand casualties. Soviet casualties were also high. Roughly 1 million soldiers and forty thousand Soviet civilians lost their lives.

The battle of Stalingrad was a crushing blow for Hitler and the turning point that led to Germany's ultimate defeat. By the fall of 1945, World War II was over. The Soviet Union had suffered more casualties in the war than any other nation. But emerging from the rubble of war was a new order of national alliances, and the Soviet Union would be a major force in the new era that was about to dawn.

CHAPTER FOUR

The Cold War

On the southern coast of Crimea on the Black Sea lies the city of Yalta, its temperate climate and abundant sunshine making it a popular summer resort since the nineteenth century. Just west of the city is Livadia Palace, which once served as the summer residence of Czar Nicholas II. As World War II in Europe was drawing to a close in February 1945, British prime minister Winston Churchill, US president Franklin Roosevelt, and Soviet leader Joseph Stalin arrived at Livadia. The three leaders were there to decide the future of the postwar world.

During eight days of negotiations, they made decisions that would affect millions around the world. Stalin agreed that the Soviet Union would join America's Pacific war against Japan, and Roosevelt gained support for his plan of an international security organization, which would become the United Nations. The most important decisions, however, were those affecting the future of Germany, Poland, and the rest of Europe. Germany would be divided into four Allied occupation zones: the American, British, and Soviet zones, plus a French zone carved from the American and British areas.

The fate of Poland was an important topic at the conference. Since Germany had attacked Russia through Poland in two world wars, Stalin wanted it to act as a barrier between his country and possible further attacks from

"[We agree to assist the] states of Europe to solve by democratic means their pressing political and economic problems . . . and [pledge] to the earliest possible establishment through free elections of Governments responsive to the will of the people."[23]

—The Yalta agreement between the United States, Great Britain, and the Soviet Union

Western Europe. Britain and the United States believed that Poland (and other Eastern European nations) should be free to determine their own futures. At the end of the Yalta Conference, the three leaders signed the Declaration of Liberated Europe, agreeing to "[assist the] states of Europe to solve by democratic means their pressing political and economic problems . . . and [pledge] to the earliest possible establishment through free elections of Governments responsive to the will of the people."[23] While all three heads of state signed the declaration, Stalin would soon reveal his true plans for the Soviet Union's place in the new Europe. When Vyacheslav Molotov questioned him about the pledge to allow free elections, Stalin replied, "Never mind. We'll do it in our own way later."[24]

The World After War

Roosevelt and Churchill hoped that Stalin would keep the pledge of allowing European nations to hold democratic elections. But the reality of Stalin's duplicity was soon revealed when he established a Communist government in Poland in November 1949. After the war he extended the Soviet Union's sphere of influence over much of the rest of Eastern Europe. Backed by the might of the Red Army and achieved by rigged elections, Stalin installed Communist governments in Bulgaria, Czechoslovakia, East Germany, Hungary, and Romania. This new Eastern bloc of Communist nations made clear the Soviet Union's intentions for global domination.

Harry Truman, who became US president after the sudden death of Roosevelt in April 1945, inherited a world fraught with danger. The two most powerful nations in the postwar world, the United States and the Soviet Union, were locked in an ideological struggle that became known as the Cold War. The agreement

In February 1945, British prime minister Winston Churchill (left), US president Franklin Roosevelt (center), and Soviet leader Joseph Stalin (right) met in Yalta. The purpose of the meeting was to decide the future of the postwar world.

at Yalta that had promised free elections in Europe was ignored by Stalin, whose quest for expanding Soviet influence had put most of Eastern Europe behind an "iron curtain" of communism. In 1947 Truman established a policy whereby the United States would help any democratic nation resist the advance of communism. Called the Truman Doctrine, it was an effort to prevent the Soviet Union from further spreading its Communist ideology.

The lines of the Cold War between the democratic West, led by the United States, and the Communist East, led by the Soviet Union, were drawn. Stalin would be first to test the strength of those lines.

Blockading Berlin

The German capital of Berlin, like the partitioning of the nation itself, was divided into Soviet eastern and Allied western sectors. Berlin was located entirely within Germany's Soviet-controlled Eastern zone. Stalin saw an opportunity to solidify his hold over

Germany by forcing the Allied occupation forces out of West Berlin and, ultimately, all of West Germany. On June 24, 1948, the Soviets halted all road, rail, and river traffic going into West Berlin in the hopes of starving the city into submission.

In response, the United States and Great Britain established the Berlin Airlift, flying over the blockade to deliver supplies to the city's 2 million residents. Within days, cargo planes were carrying food, fuel, medicine, and other supplies into West Berlin, landing a 2.5-ton (2.27 metric ton) load every eight minutes. Soon larger planes were put into service, delivering up to 5,000 tons (4,536 metric tons) a day. The success of the Berlin Airlift shocked Stalin, and on May 11, 1949, the Soviets removed the barriers and ended the blockade. More than 2.3 million tons (2.1 million metric tons) of cargo had been delivered to Berlin. The first Cold War test of wills between a Communist state and a capitalist democracy resulted in the Soviets backing down. But the rivalry would only grow more dangerous as the Cold War continued.

A cargo plane carrying supplies comes in for a landing. When the Soviet Union blockaded West Berlin in June 1948, the United States and Great Britain responded with an operation called the Berlin Airlift, which deliver supplies to the city's 2 million residents.

The Soviet Union's Iron Curtain

When World War II ended in Europe in 1945, it left the globe divided between Eastern nations dominated by the Soviet Union and Western nations led by the United States. This ideological rift was not a physical obstacle (except for the concrete wall that separated East and West Berlin from 1961 to 1989), but it was just as effective as a real barrier. In 1946 former British prime minister Winston Churchill used a term that aptly described the newly divided world. During a speech at Westminster College in Fulton, Missouri, Churchill spoke the famous words that vividly captured the postwar divide.

> From Stettin in the Baltic to Trieste in the Adriatic, an iron curtain has descended across the Continent. Behind that line lie all the capitals of the ancient states of Central and Eastern Europe. Warsaw, Berlin, Prague, Vienna, Budapest, Belgrade, Bucharest and Sofia, all these famous cities and the populations around them lie in what I must call the Soviet sphere, and all are subject in one form or another, not only to Soviet influence but to a very high and, in many cases, increasing measure of control from Moscow.

Quoted in America's National Churchill Museum, "Sinews of Peace, 1946," 2022. www.nationalchurchillmuseum.org.

The Nuclear Arms Race

When the war in Europe ended in May 1945, the United States was still locked in bitter combat with Japan. In August 1945 US aircraft dropped atomic bombs on Hiroshima and Nagasaki in Japan, bringing an end to World War II in the Pacific. A few weeks before the bombing, Truman had informed Stalin about America's "new weapon of unusual destructive force,"[25] but Stalin did not seem surprised. Unknown to the president, spies had stolen secrets of the bomb, and the Soviet Union was developing its own atomic weapon.

Building an atomic bomb was a massive undertaking for the Soviet Union, but Stalin was obsessed with catching up to the United States. "Ask for whatever you like," Stalin told his scientists. "You won't be refused."[26] Funds that could have been used to improve Soviet agriculture and other industries were diverted to the bomb program. Prisoners were forced to labor in uranium mines without any regard for their safety or health.

On August 29, 1949, the Soviet Union successfully tested its first atomic bomb. Until then, the United States was the world's only nuclear power. Now the two nations escalated their rivalry, each developing their own hydrogen bomb, a nuclear weapon with even greater destructive power. By 1953 the Soviet Union had 120 nuclear bombs, about one-tenth of America's stockpile. That same year, as the USSR continued to build up its nuclear arsenal, a shocking death rocked the Soviet Union, with implications for the entire world.

Succeeding Stalin

On March 1, 1953, Stalin was found nearly unconscious on the floor of his dacha (summer home) after suffering a cerebral hemorrhage. For the next several days, a group of physicians attended to him, but Stalin's health had deteriorated too much. At 9:50 p.m. on March 5, Joseph Stalin died. Despite Stalin's thirty-year reign of terror over the Soviet Union, thousands of Soviet citizens turned out to see him lying in state. After his funeral, Stalin's body was entombed in Lenin's Mausoleum in Moscow.

Like Lenin before him, Stalin had not chosen a successor. The role ultimately fell to fifty-nine-year-old Nikita Khrushchev, a longtime supporter of Stalin's rule. In September 1953 Khrushchev became first secretary of the Communist Party Central Committee. In 1956 he stunned the party with an address that came to be known as the Secret Speech (because it was intended only for the party elite). In it, Khrushchev condemned the Great Terror and asserted that Stalin had replaced the ideals of communism with a cult of personality. Despite efforts to limit the number of people who heard Khrushchev's comments, the speech circulated widely. Soviet citizens who had previously expressed admiration for Stalin were forced to reconsider their position. Portraits and statues of Stalin were destroyed, and Stalingrad underwent a name change to Volgograd. In 1961 Stalin's body was removed

In 1961 Soviet leader Nikita Khrushchev ordered the building of a wall to isolate West Berlin from East Berlin. The wall was intended to prevent Western ideas and ways of life from influencing people in the Communist zone.

from Lenin's Mausoleum and interred in a less prominent location. Despite Khrushchev's criticism of Stalin's methods, however, he would use those same tactics in putting down rebellions in Soviet satellite nations Poland and Hungary.

In a speech later that year at a meeting of Western diplomats, Khrushchev indignantly announced, "We will bury you!"[27] Although the context indicated that Khrushchev was referring to the economic rivalry between East and West, many believed it was a threat to the very existence of Western nations, and a sign that the Cold War was far from over.

The Soviet Union in Space

As the 1960s began, the world was kept on edge by the rivalry between the Soviet Union and the United States. The Soviet nuclear arsenal still lagged behind America's (it would not surpass

US stockpiles until 1978). Scientists in both nations were developing intercontinental ballistic missiles (ICBMs) that could deliver nuclear warheads over thousands of miles. In October 1957 the Soviet Union had used such a missile to launch the first artificial Earth satellite. For three months the satellite, named *Sputnik 1*, orbited Earth every ninety-six minutes, transmitting a regular beep-beep that could be heard on terrestrial radios worldwide.

The success of *Sputnik 1* gave the Soviet Union bragging rights over the United States, which would not put a satellite in orbit until almost four months later. Space continued to be a realm where the Soviet Union garnered more firsts. One month after *Sputnik 1*, a dog named Laika became the first animal in orbit, followed in 1961 by cosmonaut Yuri Gagarin, the first human being in space. Soviet space achievements struck fear into the hearts of the American public, which reasoned that if the Soviets could launch a satellite into space, they could also launch a nuclear warhead toward the United States.

Cold War Rivals

When the Cold War split the world into two geopolitical coalitions, it also divided the world's military forces into two armed camps: the North Atlantic Treaty Organization (NATO) and the Warsaw Pact. With tensions between the Communist East and democratic West creating an atmosphere of perpetual uncertainty, the Soviet Union and the United States had to prepare for the possibility that the Cold War could turn hot, by accident or design.

The United States and twenty-nine other Western nations established NATO on April 4, 1949. The key point of the treaty was the concept of mutual defense: if any NATO member nation were attacked, it would be considered an attack on all members. NATO's armed forces would respond to any such occurrence with a coordinated military effort.

In response, in 1955 the Soviet Union created its own military alliance called the Warsaw Pact. It consisted of the Soviet Union and seven other Communist bloc nations. The Warsaw Pact's mission was similar to NATO's, providing collective security for its member nations. But it also helped the Soviet Union maintain firm control over its satellite nations.

The two alliances never directly fought each other. The Warsaw Pact was dissolved in 1991.

Cold War Crises

As the Cold War deepened, two crises tipped the two nations ever closer to nuclear war. In 1960 an American U-2 spy plane was shot down while flying a reconnaissance mission over the Soviet Union. Khrushchev was furious and accused the United States of espionage. Two weeks later he abruptly cut short a Paris summit meeting when he demanded but did not receive an apology from US president Dwight Eisenhower. The incident was an embarrassment to the United States, and it destroyed an easing of tensions between the two nations that had created hopes of a possible end to the Cold War.

In 1961 Khrushchev ordered the building of a concrete wall isolating West Berlin from East Berlin. The Berlin Wall was intended to prevent Western ideas and ways of life from influencing people in the Communist zone. Soviet armed guards, ditches, barbed wire, and guard dogs protected the wall, discouraging efforts to breach the barrier. Despite these obstacles, thousands managed to defect from East Germany, but many were shot to death attempting to escape. Western diplomats roundly condemned the Berlin Wall. Twenty years after it was built, British prime minister Margaret Thatcher called the wall "an ever present reminder that those who repress the liberties of our Eastern neighbors seek also to extinguish our own."[28]

As the Berlin Wall sparked concern among West Germans, a new crisis was about to unfold closer to the United States. On October 14, 1962, a US spy plane flying over Cuba photographed Soviet medium- and long-range ballistic missiles and launch facilities. Such weapons could deliver nuclear warheads to nearly all of the continental United States, a threat that the United States could not tolerate. With thirty more Soviet cargo ships headed for Cuba, US president John Kennedy initiated a naval blockade to stop the approaching vessels. For thirteen days the world teetered on the brink of nuclear war, until Khrushchev finally agreed to remove the missiles. Kennedy, in turn, agreed not to invade Cuba and would withdraw US missiles from Turkey, which, according to Khrushchev, posed a similar threat to the Soviet Union.

Khrushchev's Reforms

Despite the Cold War crises, Khrushchev managed to instill his own brand of communism in the Soviet Union, a series of reforms that came to be known as the Khrushchev Thaw. Turning away from the brutality of the Stalin years, he freed millions of political prisoners from the gulags and directed Soviet industry to increase the manufacture of consumer goods. Khrushchev encouraged Soviet society to embrace art, films, books, fashion, musical performances, and other cultural pursuits. In foreign relations, Khrushchev rejected the traditional Communist notion that war between communism and capitalism was inevitable, and he met with leaders of China, Yugoslavia, and the United States. "The Soviet Union," Khrushchev said in a 1958 speech in Budapest, Hungary, "offers the capitalist countries to compete in raising living standards rather than in the arms race."[29] As encouraging as the idea of peaceful coexistence was, however, Khrushchev's reforms did not last.

> **"The Soviet Union offers the capitalist countries to compete in raising living standards rather than in the arms race."[29]**
>
> **—Nikita Khrushchev**

Khrushchev was not a typical Soviet leader. His personality alternated between shouting threats at and joking with colleagues and foreign leaders. Both inside and outside the Soviet Union, he was often seen as a buffoon wearing ill-fitting suits, a dullard with limited diplomatic and intellectual skills. Khrushchev's agricultural reforms failed to improve continuing food shortages, and his capitulation in the Cuban missile crisis was an embarrassing stain on his record. By 1964 Khrushchev knew he would soon be forced to retire. He told a high-ranking party official, "I'm old and tired. . . . I won't put up a fight."[30]

Khrushchev resigned on October 14, 1964. He left Moscow to live the rest of his life in relative obscurity. The Khrushchev Thaw was over, and soon Soviet tanks would again be rolling across Eastern Europe.

CHAPTER FIVE

Collapse and Rebirth

On the night of August 20, 1968, 165,000 troops and more than 4,000 tanks from the Soviet Union and other Communist bloc nations invaded Czechoslovakia, a country that had been under Soviet control for two decades. The attack was a response to liberal reforms begun by the country's president, Alexander Dubček. The invading forces quickly defeated Czechoslovakia's army, and Dubček was arrested. The Soviet Union asserted that such military action was justified against any Eastern European Communist nation that strayed too far from Communist philosophy. This policy became known as the Brezhnev Doctrine, named for the man who succeeded Khrushchev.

Leonid Brezhnev became the Soviet Union's Communist Party first secretary (later changed to general secretary) in 1964 after orchestrating Khrushchev's removal from power. A soldier in the Red Army during World War II, Brezhnev's approach to governing seemed closer to Stalin's than Khrushchev's. Brezhnev began reversing Khrushchev's reforms and put an end to his predecessor's de-Stalinization plan. Protest movements were suppressed by the KGB (formerly the NKVD), which isolated dissidents in facilities that were called psychiatric hospitals but served as abusive prisons.

Stagnation and Détente

While Khrushchev's policies did little to improve the Soviet standard of living, Brezhnev's administration drove the nation into serious economic trouble. The 1970s saw the Soviet Union's economy in a slow decline. Manufacturing based on government quotas rather than market demand created consumer goods that no one wanted. Massive military spending in order to keep up with the United States took up much of the Soviet Union's economic resources. Agriculture, a persistent Soviet problem, remained unable to properly feed Soviet citizens. Brezhnev's weak reform efforts did little to relieve his nation's economic problems, and this period came to be known as the Era of Stagnation.

The Soviet Union fared better in foreign policy matters under Brezhnev. Beginning in 1969 a new period called détente (French for "relaxation") began to ease Cold War tensions. It was a decade of improved economic, political, and military relations between the Soviet Union and the United States. Both nations had built up their nuclear stockpiles in the 1960s and 1970s, leaving the world fearing another nuclear confrontation like the Cuban missile crisis. In 1969 US and Soviet diplomats began Strategic Arms Limitation Talks (SALT) to discuss the problem of nuclear weapons. Signed in 1972, SALT I placed a temporary limit on US and Soviet nuclear missiles. A subsequent agreement in 1979, SALT II, permanently restricted ICBMs and bombers and limited production of new types of nuclear weapons.

With the SALT II agreement, a more peaceful world seemed to be on the horizon. But a new Soviet act of aggression led the United States to refuse to ratify the agreement.

Afghanistan Invasion

In December 1979 the Soviet Union invaded Afghanistan in support of its Communist government's struggle against anti-Communist Muslim rebels called mujahideen. Soviet airborne troops secured the Afghan capital of Kabul, and armored divi-

Members of Afghanistan's mujahideen pose with their automatic weapons. When Soviet troops invaded their country in 1979, the anti-Communist mujahideen fought against them.

sions crushed resistance fighters. The Soviet action prompted global protests and shattered the atmosphere of détente between East and West. The quick occupation of the country soon turned into a quagmire for the Soviets, a seemingly unwinnable war against the mujahideen. In nine years of fighting, an estimated 500,000 to 2 million Afghan civilians had died.

On February 15, 1989, the last Soviet occupation troops left Afghanistan. By that time, the Soviet Union had a new leader and was on its way to yet another profound transformation.

Gorbachev Takes Charge

Brezhnev died of a heart attack on November 10, 1982. He was followed by two successors, Yuri Andropov and Konstantin Chernenko, whose short terms had little effect on the Soviet Union's ongoing problems. After Chernenko's death in 1985, Mikhail Gorbachev was elected general secretary of the Soviet Union. His first task was to introduce two major reform projects to reverse the economic stagnation that had plagued the nation since Brezhnev's rule. Under glasnost, meaning "openness," the Soviet Union would become more forthcoming in sharing information with the world and encouraging freedom of speech and the press. Perestroika, or "restructuring," included reforms such as secret ballots, multiple parties represented in elections, a new parliament, and moving the Soviet Union closer to a capitalist-style economy.

In 1987 Gorbachev wrote that perestroika "is designed to bring society to new frontiers and raise it to a qualitatively new level. We

"[Perestroika] is designed to bring society to new frontiers and raise it to a qualitatively new level. We will have to make sacrifices, which will not be easy."[31]

—Mikhail Gorbachev

shall have to make sacrifices, which will not be easy."[31] However, after enduring decades of sacrifices, the Soviet people did not look kindly on new ones. Many bureaucrats in the Communist Party resisted the new reforms as well, fearing the loss of their power in the government. As Gorbachev labored to make his dual reform programs successful, his nation was heading toward an ultimate crisis that would rock the Soviet Union and the world.

The Collapse of the Soviet Union

As the Soviet Union became more open, Soviet critics gained the freedom to condemn the disparity between the lives of ordinary citizens and high-ranking members of the Communist Party. Free elections further helped draw the Soviet Union toward the establishment of a democratic government. In 1990 the nations that had been forced by the Soviets into submission began to assert their freedom. On December 8, 1991, the leaders of Belarus, Russia, and Ukraine signed the Belovezh Accords, which stated that "the Union of Soviet Socialist Republics as a subject of international law and a geopolitical reality no longer exists."[32] The agreement established the Commonwealth of Independent States (CIS), successor to the Soviet Union. The Baltic states of Estonia, Latvia, and Lithuania were the first to declare their independence; eventually, all republics under the rule of the Soviet Union became autonomous. The once-united alliance of Soviet republics had become fifteen independent states.

On December 25, 1991, Gorbachev, in a televised address from the Kremlin, resigned as president of the Soviet Union. At 7:32 p.m. the red hammer-and-sickle flag of the Soviet Union was lowered from a flagpole atop the Kremlin and replaced by the red, white, and blue tricolor of the Russian Federation. After sixty-nine years under the banner of communism, Russia was about to emerge as a part of the democratic world.

Russia Reborn

As Gorbachev faded from the political scene, sixty-year-old Boris Yeltsin became the first democratically elected president of the Russian Federation. He initiated numerous fiscal policies all at once, a tactic often called economic shock therapy, to try to stimulate the Russian economy. "Everyone will find life harder for approximately six months," he proclaimed, "then prices will fall."[33] But Yeltsin's prediction fell flat as food prices skyrocketed, shortages continued, and in late 1993 inflation topped 1,000 percent. The Russian parliament's opposition to these reforms led Yeltsin to dissolve the legislative body and call for new elections.

Along with its economic problems, in 1994 Russia became embroiled in a two-year war to bring Chechnya, a republic that had separated from Russia in 1991, back into line. Unable to defeat Chechen forces and experiencing nearly universal condemnation at home, Russia signed a cease-fire in 1996.

Russia's Tiny Foe

Chechnya is a mountainous republic in southwestern Russia with a long history of resistance to Soviet rule. Shortly after the breakup of the Soviet Union, Chechnya declared its independence. The new Russian government feared Chechnya's declaration might motivate other republics to also seek freedom. It mounted an invasion with air strikes and ground troops, destroying much of the republic and killing some one hundred thousand people. But Russia could not eliminate its determined adversary; a truce ended the fighting in 1996 but left the future of Chechnya uncertain.

The Chechen rebels were not finished. They employed guerrilla tactics to bomb Russian apartment buildings, killing hundreds, and in 2002 took some seven hundred hostages in a Moscow theater, many of whom died in a rescue operation. Calling the Chechens terrorists, President Vladimir Putin sent troops back into Chechnya. More years of combat followed, until a Russian-backed president was installed in Chechnya in 2007.

Some observers see similarities to Chechnya in the Russian war in Ukraine. "There are some pretty disturbing parallels," comments journalist Thomas de Waal. "The use of heavy artillery, the indiscriminate attacking of an urban center. They bring back some pretty terrible memories."

Quoted in Greg Myre, "Russia's Wars in Chechnya Offer a Grim Warning of What Could Be in Ukraine," *Weekend Edition Saturday*, NPR, March 12, 2022. www.npr.org.

Despite his disappointing reforms and growing unpopularity, in 1996 Yeltsin was reelected president. Still, he could not slow the tide of disapproval, even going so far as to fire his entire cabinet in 1998. Also coping with continuing health problems, he knew his days as Russia's leader were numbered. Finally, on December 31, 1999, Yeltsin resigned, thrusting Vladimir Putin into the role of acting president of Russia.

Putin's Reforms

In his political career, Putin had been a KGB operative, the deputy mayor of St. Petersburg, and Yeltsin's prime minister. Putin's new position as the leader of Russia was confirmed in a general election held on March 26, 2000, in which he won his first four-year term with more than 53 percent of the votes. In his inaugural address, Putin proclaimed, "We want our Russia to be a free, prosperous, flourishing, strong and civilized country, a country that its citizens are proud of and that is respected internationally."[34] Putin's goal of achieving economic prosperity was a daunting task. According to the Center for Strategic and International Studies, Russia was effectively bankrupt when Putin took office. Putin instituted progressive tax reform and simplified regulations that had hindered the development of small businesses. Russia's economy rebounded, driven in part by rising prices of Russian oil.

> **"We want our Russia to be a free, prosperous, flourishing, strong and civilized country, a country that its citizens are proud of and that is respected internationally."[34]**
>
> **—Vladimir Putin**

After serving two terms as president, Putin was constitutionally barred from running for a third term. First Deputy Prime Minister Dmitry Medvedev was elected president in 2008, and he immediately appointed Putin prime minister. For four years the two men shared power together in what has been dubbed a "tandemocracy." Medvedev also made a deal that assured that Putin could run for a third term, and in 2012 Putin was once more elected as Russia's president.

When Dmitry Medvedev (right) was elected as Russia's president in 2008, he immediately appointed Vladimir Putin (left) as prime minister. The two men would share power for the next four years.

Foreign Affairs

During his third term, Putin prepared to return Russia to its Cold War status as a global power, and Ukraine became a symbol of that goal. One of the founding republics of the Soviet Union, Ukraine had declared its independence in 1991 with the USSR's collapse. But Putin had always viewed Ukraine as a part of Russia, and he lamented what in his view was an "artificial division of Russians and Ukrainians."[35] In February 2014 Ukraine's president was removed from office, and a Russian military force occupied Crimea, a peninsula in the south of Ukraine. A month later Russian sympathizers (aided by Russian troops and tanks) took control of two provinces in the Donbas region of eastern Ukraine. Despite peace negotiations, hostilities continued for eight years until full-scale war erupted.

On February 24, 2022, Russian forces invaded Ukraine, attacking military and civilian targets with missiles, helicopters, tanks, and ground troops. Russia's hopes for a quick victory were soon dashed as the Ukrainian military proved surprisingly effective in countering the invasion. The military prevented Russian troops from seizing Kyiv, Ukraine's capital city, and soon recaptured many areas that were occupied by Russian forces. Ukrainian civilians armed with hand-thrown incendiary bombs called Molotov cocktails helped their military damage or destroy more than fourteen hundred Russian tanks. Military officials worldwide derided Russia's inept handling of the war as supply problems, fuel and food shortages, and desertions crippled the army's ability to fight effectively.

Amid global outrage against the unprovoked invasion, nations imposed sanctions on Russian industries, government entities, financial institutions, and powerful individuals. As a result, the Russian economy showed a major drop in its gross domestic product (a measure of financial health), while inflation spiked to more than 20 percent two months after the invasion began. More disconcerting, however, is the cost of the war in human suffering in Ukraine. Russian forces have willfully damaged or destroyed schools, hospitals, apartment buildings, and other civilian structures. Damage to infrastructure created serious civilian hardships

Ukrainian forces attack a column of Russian tanks and armored vehicles in March 2022. Russia's hopes of a quick victory in its invasion of Ukraine were soon dashed, as Ukrainian troops and civilians proved unexpectedly effective in countering Russian forces.

The Oligarchs of Russia

In June 2022 a boat named *Amadea* was seized by a group of US and international law enforcement agencies known as Task Force KleptoCapture. "Boat" hardly describes the vessel, however. The *Amadea* is a 348-foot (106 m) superyacht, worth some $325 million and, until its confiscation, owned by one of Russia's wealthiest businesspersons, known as oligarchs.

Oligarchs first appeared in Russia shortly after the collapse of the Soviet Union in 1991. As the nation evolved into a capitalist, free-market economy, corrupt businesspeople manipulated the fledgling system to their advantage, accumulating enormous wealth in the process. The oligarchs gained political power and influence as well. Some oligarchs have close ties with Russian president Vladimir Putin, going back to his days as a KGB agent.

As international sanctions were imposed on Russia after the invasion of Ukraine, the assets of the richest oligarchs became fair game. Besides luxury yachts like the *Amadea*, lavish mansions and private jets were seized and more than $300 billion in bank accounts frozen. Meanwhile, the *Amadea* is now moored in San Diego, California.

to the Ukrainian populace as power, water, sanitation, and delivery of food and medicine were disrupted. In September 2022 the United Nations reported that the war had caused 14,059 Ukrainian civilian casualties (5,767 killed and 8,292 injured), although officials believe the real numbers are likely higher. In October 2022 the United Nations noted that almost 8 million Ukrainian refugees had sought safety in other European nations. By November both Russian and Ukrainian forces had suffered some 120,000 military casualties each, according to chair of the US Joint Chiefs of Staff General Mark Milley.

Throughout the twentieth century, Russia had many incarnations: from the often-brutal reign of revolutionary communism, through superpower status during the Cold War, to a modern-day republic struggling to cope with its past and find a way forward to a new future. What that future holds depends on Russia's political leadership and its willingness to integrate into the twenty-first century as a strong and peaceful member of the global community.

SOURCE NOTES

Introduction: Russia: Vision of a Communist World

1. Karl Marx and Friedrich Engels, *The Communist Manifesto*. New York: Penguin, 1985, p. 121.

Chapter One: Empire and Revolution

2. Quoted in Greg King, *The Court of the Last Tsar: Pomp, Power and Pageantry in the Reign of Nicholas II*. Hoboken, NJ: Wiley, 2006, p. 375.
3. Quoted in Yulia Afanasynko, "The Khodynka Tragedy: A Coronation Ruined by a Stampede," Russia Beyond, July 23, 2020. www.rbth.com.
4. Quoted in Orlando Figes, *Revolutionary Russia: 1891–1991*. New York: Metropolitan, 2014, p. 10.
5. Quoted in Figes, *Revolutionary Russia*, p. 9.
6. Figes, *Revolutionary Russia*, p. 16.
7. Quoted in Peter Kurth, *Tsar: The Lost World of Nicholas and Alexandra.* Boston: Madison, 1995, p. 81.
8. Quoted in Figes, *Revolutionary Russia*, p. 30.
9. Quoted in Michael Farquhar, *Secret Lives of the Tsars: Three Centuries of Autocracy, Debauchery, Betrayal, Murder, and Madness from Romanov Russia*. New York: Random House, 2014, p. 257.

Chapter Two: Revolutionary Changes

10. Quoted in Victor Sebestyen, *Lenin: The Man, the Dictator, and the Master of Terror*. New York: Pantheon, 2017, p. 288.
11. Quoted in Catherine Merridale, *Lenin on the Train*. New York: Metropolitan, 2017, pp. 223–24.
12. Quoted in Progress Publishers, *Lenin's Collected Works*, vol. 26. Moscow: Progress, 1972, pp. 19–21.
13. Quoted in Progress Publishers, *Lenin's Collected Works*, p. 236.
14. Quoted in Sebestyen, *Lenin*, p. 21.
15. Quoted in Orlando Figes, *A People's Tragedy: The Russian Revolution, 1891–1924*. New York: Penguin, 1996, p. 536.
16. Quoted in Second All-Russia Congress of Soviets of Workers' and Soldiers' Deputies, "Report on Land, October 26 (November 8)," Marxists Internet Archive. www.marxists.org.

17. Quoted in Erin Blakemore, "How the Red Terror Set a Macabre Course for the Soviet Union," National Geographic, September 2, 2020. www.nationalgeographic.com.

Chapter Three: An Era of Terror and War

18. V.I. Lenin, "Letter to the Congress," Marxists Internet Archive. www.marxists.org.
19. Quoted in Derek Watson, *Molotov: A Biography*. New York: Palgrave Macmillan, 2005, p. 108.
20. Quoted in Robert Service, *Stalin: A Biography*. Cambridge, MA: Belknap, 2006, p. 266.
21. Quoted in Robert Conquest, *Harvest of Sorrow: Soviet Collectivization and the Terror-Famine*. New York: Oxford University Press, 1986, p. 245.
22. Quoted in Simon Sebag Montefiore, *Stalin: The Court of the Red Tsar*. New York: Knopf, 2004, p. 311.

Chapter Four: The Cold War

23. Quoted in Wilson Center, "Yalta Conference Agreement, Declaration of a Liberated Europe," 2013. www.digitalarchive.wilsoncenter.org.
24. Quoted in Simon Berthon and Joanna Potts, *Warlords: An Extraordinary Re-creation of World War II Through the Eyes and Minds of Hitler, Churchill, Roosevelt and Stalin*. Cambridge, MA: Da Capo, 2006, p. 289.
25. Quoted in Kristine Phillips, "'He Is Honest—but Smart as Hell': When Truman Met Stalin," *Washington Post*, July 17, 2018. www.washingtonpost.com.
26. Quoted in David Holloway, *Stalin and the Bomb: The Soviet Union and Atomic Energy, 1939–1956*. New Haven, CT: Yale University Press, 1994, p. 132.
27. Quoted in William Taubman, *Khrushchev: The Man and His Era*. New York: Norton, 2003, p. 427.
28. Quoted in John Tagliabue, "Mrs. Thatcher Visits the Berlin Wall," *New York Times*, October 30, 1982. www.nytimes.com.
29. N.S. Khrushchev, *For Victory in the Peaceful Competition with Capitalism*. Moscow: Foreign Languages Publishing House, 1959, p. 262.
30. Quoted in Taubman, *Khrushchev*, p. 13.

Chapter Five: Collapse and Rebirth

31. Mikhail Gorbachev, *Perestroika: New Thinking for Our Country and the World*. New York: Harper & Row, 1987, p. 53.
32. European Commission for Democracy Through Law, "Agreements Establishing the Commonwealth of Independent States," Council of Europe, September 8, 1994. www.venice.coe.int.
33. Quoted in Jonathan Steele, "Boris Yeltsin," *The Guardian* (Manchester, UK), April 23, 2007. www.theguardian.com.
34. Quoted in Reuters, "Putin's Inaugural Address: 'We Believe in Our Strength,'" *New York Times*, May 8, 2000. www.nytimes.com.
35. Vladimir Putin, "On the Historical Unity of Russians and Ukrainians," July 12, 2021. www.en.kremlin.ru.

ORGANIZATION AND WEBSITES

In Defense of October
www.bolshevik.info
This website is dedicated to the Russian Revolution and the philosophies of Bolshevism. Included are videos, timelines, biographies, and reading guides that present in detail the revolution from its beginning to the establishment of the communist state.

John F. Kennedy Presidential Library and Museum
www.jfklibrary.org
Visitors to this website can learn about US and Soviet relations in the most dangerous period of the Cold War. It includes information on the origins of the Cold War, the role Berlin played in the conflict, and the missile crisis that brought the world to the edge of nuclear war.

Library of Congress: Revelations from the Russian Archives
www.loc.gov/exhibits/archives
Information about the Soviet Union from the Revolution of 1917 to the era of perestroika. The site contains details of Stalin's reign of terror, persecution of intellectuals and Jews, and the Ukrainian famine. Also features photographs and original Communist documents.

Marxists Internet Archive
www.marxists.org
A comprehensive website that covers the history and philosophy of Marxism. Contains a large library of articles, a history archive, audiobooks, and a comprehensive Marxist encyclopedia.

North Atlantic Treaty Organization (NATO)
www.nato.int
NATO's website includes an online multimedia experience with information about its mission and structure; an interactive map; videos, documents, and posters about NATO's history; and details about its student internship program.

Russia Beyond
www.rbth.com
A comprehensive website created by the official Russian state news agency. It presents information (usually characterized by the West as propaganda) on all aspects of Russian culture, scientific achievements, history, and the modern Russian lifestyle.

Russian Government Website
http://government.ru/en
This is the official website of the Russian government, with information on current affairs, news articles, and a link to Vladimir Putin's presidential website.

Seventeen Moments in Russian History
https://soviethistory.msu.edu
This is a multimedia library of primary sources on Russian history. The exhaustive archive contains images, video clips, music, and primary texts, as well as a glossary and biographies of more than six hundred people in Russian history.

FOR FURTHER RESEARCH

Books

John Allen, *Vladimir Putin: Russia's Autocratic Ruler*. San Diego, CA: ReferencePoint, 2023.

Budd Bailey, *The Formation and Dissolution of the Soviet Union*. New York: Cavendish Square, 2019.

Craig E. Blohm, *The Unprovoked War: Russia's Invasion of Ukraine*. San Diego, CA: ReferencePoint, 2023.

Orlando Figes, *The Story of Russia*. New York: Metropolitan, 2022.

Erik Richardson, *NATO, the Warsaw Pact, and the Iron Curtain*. New York: Cavendish Square, 2018.

Philip Short, *Putin*. New York: Henry Holt, 2022.

Internet Sources

Alessandra Bonomolo and William McLennan, "Inside the Capture of a Russian Oligarch's Superyacht," BBC News, November 11, 2022. www.bbc.com.

Joshua Hammer, "Vladimir Lenin's Return Journey to Russia Changed the World Forever," *Smithsonian*, March 2017. www.smithsonian.com.

Nathan Hodge, "History Wars: What Putin's Attempts to Rewrite the Past Say About Russia's Future," CNN, December 24, 2021. www.cnn.com.

Serhii Plokhy, "Lenin vs Stalin: Their Showdown over the Birth of the USSR," History.com, February 1, 2019. www.history.com.

Oleg Yegorov, "The Fall of the Winter Palace: How the Bolsheviks Took Power 100 Years Ago," Russia Beyond, November 7, 2017. www.rbth.com.

Cathy Young, "How Freedom and Dreams of a 'Normal Life' Died in Post-Cold-War Russia," Cato Institute, March 14, 2022. www.cato.org.

INDEX